Having Faith

For Others

Curry R. Blake

Copyright © 2018 by Curry R. Blake
All Rights Reserved

Published by
CHRISTIAN REALITY BOOKS
P.O. Box 742947
Dallas TX 75374
1-888-293-6591

Unless otherwise noted, all Scripture quotations are taken from the King James Bible.

This book or parts thereof may not be reproduced in any form without express written permission of Curry Blake.

Printed in the United States of America.

Having Faith for Others

We are going to be dealing with having faith for others. This area tends to be the one that we are criticized in the most. It is amazing that we would get criticized for wanting to believe God for other people. If someone is going to give somebody criticism for believing God, then they need to examine their hearts, not criticize Christians for wanting to have faith for other people.

If a Christian cannot have faith for others, then all intercession is useless, because everything has to be by faith. If you can't have faith in intercession and believe that the thing is coming to pass in these other people, if you can't pray in faith that it's going to be done, and if you can't have faith for them, then you're in sin by going into intercession.

Remember: whatever is not of faith is sin (Romans 14:23). You have to be able to have faith for other people or else every time you intercede in prayer, you are actually entering into sin. I know that sounds crazy, but logically, that's the way it would run.

Matthew 9:28-30,

> *28 And when he was come into the house, the blind men came to him: and Jesus saith unto them, Believe ye that I am able to do this? They said unto him, Yea, Lord.*
>
> *29 Then touched he their eyes, saying, According to your faith be it unto you.*
>
> *30 And their eyes were opened;*

Obviously, if a person has their own faith, they can be healed. That is pretty well accepted, and that is usually what all preaching on healing comes back to, which is trying to get a person to have their own faith so they can rise up in faith to a point where they can be healed. It is as if there is a certain level of faith that you have to get to before you can get healed.

Jesus talked about great faith, He talked about little faith, and He talked about no faith. However, when He described faith, the only description He gave of faith that He said would be enough to do whatever you needed was faith the size of a grain of mustard seed.

Matthew 17:20,

> *20 If ye have faith as a grain of mustard seed, ye shall say unto this mountain, Remove hence to yonder*

place; and it shall remove; and nothing shall be impossible unto you.

Most people would have us believe today that the mustard seed must be the size of a mountain. Sometimes the church does things backward, and it usually teaches everything backward. Jesus said, "If you have faith the size of a grain of mustard seed, you can cast a mountain into the ocean." The church says, "If you have faith the size of a mountain, you can cast out a mustard seed." In other words, you've got to have so much faith before you can do any little thing. In reality, it's just the opposite.

The amazing thing about it is that in the illustration which Jesus used, He used the smallest seed known. He said, "The mustard seed is the smallest of all seeds, but when it grows up, it grows into a tree big enough for all the fowls of the air to live in," yet the teaching from the church is that you have to have enough faith.

Luke 13:19,

> *19 It is like a grain of mustard seed, which a man took, and cast into his garden; and it grew, and waxed a great tree; and the fowls of the air lodged in the branches of it.*

The mustard seed is the smallest seed, and Jesus said that the smallest seed of faith will do whatever you need done. That means that you can have the smallest possible faith. If you don't have faith the size of a mustard seed, you don't have faith. You've either got faith, that is at least, the size of a mustard seed or nothing.

Then you go from faith the size of a mustard seed to little faith and then to great faith. At that point, He wasn't talking about size. He was talking about persistence, a quality of faith. He was saying faith is a seed, plant it and it will grow. It's not the size of the seed, it's that seeds grow.

The amazing thing about it is that when Jesus mentioned this mustard seed size of faith, He was saying that if you have the smallest amount of faith, you can do whatever needs to be done.

When I first started studying healing, there were a number of things that really stood out. People told us, "A person has to have enough faith to be healed." Jesus never said that. He never asked, "How much faith do you have?"

There were several times when He did say, "Your faith has healed you," but you will notice that He never told a person, "Sorry, you don't have enough faith." To the blind man He had to pray for twice, He didn't say "Man, where is your faith?" No, Jesus was the one praying. It's amazing how we have turned that around. We have put all of the responsibility on the sick person to have enough faith, and we have taken off all of the responsibility from the person who comes with the power.

When I first started realizing that, everything changed in my eyes. I had just never analyzed it before. The way I had been taught and the way I had seen it done seemed as though it took someone who was *highly anointed of God* (that was the terminology that I was raised up under) in healing to have a tremendous healing ministry. When you got in front of them to get prayed for, it didn't matter how highly anointed they were; you still had to have faith!

Now, why do I care how anointed a person is if I've got to have faith? If I've got to have faith, really how anointed that person is shouldn't matter, or if the anointing matters, then how much faith I have shouldn't matter. It at least needs to be consistent, one way or the other. I had heard all of these accolades about these people and how great and how powerful they were, but when it came down to it, I still had to have faith.

Jesus said to the two blind men: "It is according to your faith." If "according to your faith" means according to how much faith you have, which is the way most people usually preach on healing, then there should have been degrees of healing, even in Jesus' ministry. You never really see that, but sometimes you do see some progression.

Sometimes when Jesus prayed for somebody, it says that they were healed as they went. That doesn't necessarily mean that they were healed by degree as they went. It just meant that on their way home, sometime between when they left the meeting and before they got home, they were healed. It doesn't mean progression in degrees of healing. Now, we know that there are degrees of power released into a person's life, but we also know that that is based on their faith for themselves.

There are several different ways to receive healing. There are all kinds of methods. There are prayer cloths, there is anointing with oil, and other kinds of ways, but it really comes down to two things. Either you've got to go off and get it for yourself by doing things such as reading, studying, praying, and fasting, or you go to another person, and they get it for you.

To get healing for yourself, at some point you're going to have to get in front of God, just you and God with no third person. Then, if you don't get it for yourself, you get with someone who can get it for you. That's where we get a lot of criticism, because they say that we can't do that. The amazing thing about it is that some have made an entire doctrine out of something Jesus never said. I know this doesn't shock most of you, because we've gone through several doctrines like that.

Obviously, if a person has their own faith they can be healed, which is the best situation. It is always better for you to get healing for yourself than to go to somebody else to get it. If you go to somebody else, you never know if they are operating on all eight cylinders. You're gambling and hoping that they are up to par, and that they are with God and that it's enough to get it done for you.

It's always better not to be a spiritual hitchhiker and expect everyone else to get everything for you. Now, that being said, if you need help, then you ought to be able to get to somebody who can get you help. If you can't get it for yourself, you're probably not going to be able to help other people get it, either. If we want to be a blessing to others, then we ought to be able to get it for ourselves so that we can give it away to others.

That's not to say that if you need help, just stick it out, and don't go to anybody. I know that there are degrees of growth, and there's a process of growth to where you say, "This time I'm just going to get it for myself." I agree; I've done that myself, but I'm also saying that if it doesn't work after a period of time, get help.

The main thing is that God doesn't want you suffering for no reason. If you're going to suffer, suffer for the right reasons, but that does not include sickness and disease. Suffering job persecution is one thing, but suffering sickness and disease is not what Jesus was referring to when He said you were going to suffer persecution.

Notice what I just said about a person being able to get healing on their own. This premise, that a person can get their own healing, would also automatically mean that it is God's will that anyone and everyone be healed. It's amazing in the faith world how we talk about healing in so many different areas. You can get healed by the anointing of God, you can get healed by your own faith, or you can get healed by someone else's faith. Having faith for others is the basis of what we're talking about.

What I'm getting at is this: if it's God's will to heal you, then anybody can be healed. We've proven through *Healing is in the Atonement* that there is no person who is beyond healing. It is God's will to heal and to save every person. The word *save* means *to heal, to prosper, and to make whole*. It is not God's will that any should perish but that everyone should be saved, healed, delivered, and set free. A person can have faith for that. These are all basic things.

We go at healing from so many different ways that people ask questions. They will ask, "Can any person be healed if they have enough faith?" Yes, that would make sense. If they have enough faith, any person can be healed and can get it for themselves.

You hear all kinds of things like: "What if this thing or that thing is not God's will right now?" or "What if God's got a perfect time and a set date for your healing?" We have heard all of this, but if you have enough faith, then you can be healed.

If it is true about having enough faith to be healed, then all of the talk about generational curses can't be true. If you had a generational curse, it wouldn't matter how much faith you had. You would have to break that curse or you couldn't get healed. You're going to have to decide what's true.

People ask, "Well, what if there's sin in my life?" Sometimes it's easier to get a sinner healed than it is a saved person. Getting a sinner healed doesn't mean that they are saved. It means they're healed. It means that God showed His mercy to them, and hopefully, they'll be smart enough to turn to God, and begin to serve Him, and get saved.

What I'm trying to get across is this: if we can have faith for ourselves, then automatically we should be able to have faith for others.

Let me give you some Scriptures, and I'll prove it.

James 5:14,

> *14 Is any sick among you? let him call for the elders of the church; and let them pray over him, anointing him with oil in the name of the Lord:*
>
> *15 And the prayer of faith shall save the sick, and the Lord shall raise him up; and if he has committed sins, they shall be forgiven him.*

It starts out by saying, *"Is any sick among you? Let him call for the elders of the church."* The sick person calls for the elders of the church. *"And let them,"* the elders of the church, *"pray over him..."* Notice it doesn't say to pray <u>with</u> him; it says to pray <u>over</u> him. The sick person's job is to call for the elders to come and pray over him. *"Let them pray over him, anointing him with oil in the Name on the Lord."*

Let's take that apart. First of all, it says in verse 15, *"And the prayer of faith shall save the sick."* The *prayer of faith* is what is going to save the sick. I know that is basic, but there is a reason for this. I am trying to get this teaching out so that we can help destroy this myth and this tradition that everybody has to have their own faith. It is wrong; it limits you, and it limits God. When people say that you can't have faith for another person to be healed, what they're saying is that Jesus lied.

Jesus said that we have authority and power over all devils, over all sickness, and over all disease. If you tell me that I can't have faith for that person to be healed of that sickness, then you're telling me that I do not truly have all authority and that I don't have authority over all sickness. You are telling me that I have authority over sickness that deals with me, but not with anybody else. If that is what you're saying, you are saying that Jesus lied. The heart of religion always says, "Jesus said this, but what He really meant was that."

Every different group thinks that they are the holder of wisdom to read Jesus' mind and to tell you what He was thinking when He said that about *all* authority. They don't think He was smart enough to say what He meant, even though He was called *The Word*. You would think that He had command of the language, being called *The Word*. They tell us that He didn't mean what He said, and they want to interpret it for us.

Jesus said that we have authority over all sickness and over all devils. People say, "But, you don't have authority over those people." I know that, and I'm not taking authority over those people. I'm taking authority over that devil. I'm taking authority over that sickness. That sickness and that devil must obey me. People say, "You're overriding that person's will." No, I'm not. They're the ones asking to be healed; I'm agreeing with their will. I'm against the devil's will, and apparently, I'm against the Pharisees will who keep arguing this. Usually, the Pharisees will agree with the devil's will. It's amazing how they work together.

If I stopped right now, wouldn't that be enough? This is pretty simple. Either Jesus meant what He said or He didn't. If he said we have absolute authority over all sickness, over all disease, and over all devils, then that means that we have authority over all the enemies of God.

Let's just take it a step farther. According to the common popular teaching, people ask, "Don't all generational curses come from the sin of somebody? Aren't they let in by a sin of some sort?" Basically, what they're saying is this: "If your granddaddy or somebody committed a sin, you're paying for it, because it came down to you." I will agree that if you live in a household with alcoholism or some other type of sin, then yes, you're very likely to pick that thing up. However, the minute you do, it's not called a generational curse; it's called a sin.

Your sin is not your daddy's sin. It's your sin. It's not a generational curse; it is a personal sin. It's not something that was passed down from your granddaddy. You have the right to say yea or nay. You have a right to agree with it and say, "Yes, I'll do the thing my daddy did," or you can say, "No, I won't do it."

I could give personal examples on that, but suffice it to say that I did not walk in the same sin my dad walked in. I was an only child, so it had nowhere else to go. It's not like it jumped off onto my cousin or someone else. It had nowhere to go. I made a vow to God, and I made a decision that I would not do that, and I have never even battled that thing. The thing that held my dad has never even tempted me. Early on, I made a commitment and said, "No!" and I killed that thing in me back then.

Now, I'm going to prove to you that generational curses don't come from somebody else's sin. Even if a person does a sin and now it's their sin, then if people say they can't get healed until they get rid of the generational curse then they must know more than James did. James said, *"The prayer of faith will save the sick and the Lord will raise him up and if he hath committed sins, they shall be forgiven him."*

Notice the progression there. You don't have the right to rearrange the words in the Bible the way they're written. Let's look at the steps. First, we see if anybody is sick, and then we tell the sick person to call for the elders. The sick person calls for the elders of the church. What do the elders do? The elders pray over him *the prayer of faith.*

It says here that *the prayer of faith* shall save the sick. Now, who prayed *the prayer of faith*? The elders prayed *the prayer of faith.* The sick person called for the elders, the elders went and prayed over him, and they anointed him with oil. *The prayer of faith* that they just prayed saved the sick person; it healed him.

Then, what did the Lord do? He raised him up. What happened after the Lord raised the sick person up? Almost as an add-on, He said, *"If he has committed sins, they will be forgiven him."*

Notice that James didn't put that first. He didn't say, "If the sick person calls for the elders, and they go and pray over him, and it doesn't work, then let the elders analyze and interrogate the person and root out the generational sin. Once they get that out of the way, then the prayer of faith will take effect, and the sick person will be healed." It was very clear that the way James was telling them to minister was the way Jesus ministered. You never found Jesus digging into somebody's past and asking, "What did you do?" He never even pointed out their sins.

Even when there was an apparent sin, He said, "Who condemns you? I'm not going to condemn you. As a matter of fact, I'm telling you that your sins are forgiven." He walked up to people and said, "Your sins are forgiven." The leaders got all upset. They said, "Who can say that? Who are you? You're blaspheming." Jesus said, "What does it matter if I say your sins are forgiven or you're healed?"

Matthew 9:1-8,

> *1 And he entered into a ship, and passed over, and came into his own city.*
>
> *2 And, behold, they brought to him a man sick of the palsy, lying on a bed: and Jesus seeing their faith said unto the sick of the palsy; Son, be of good cheer; thy sins be forgiven thee.*
>
> *3 And, behold, certain of the scribes said within themselves, This man blasphemeth.*
>
> *4 And Jesus knowing their thoughts said, Wherefore think ye evil in your hearts?*
>
> *5 For whether is easier, to say, thy sins be forgiven thee; or to say, Arise, and walk?*
>
> *6 But that ye may know that the Son of man hath power on earth to forgive sins, (then saith he to the*

> sick of the palsy,) Arise, take up thy bed, and go unto thine house.
>
> 7 And he arose, and departed to his house.
>
> 8 But when the multitudes saw it, they marvelled, and glorified God, which had given such power unto men.

Jesus said, *"Wherefore think ye evil in your hearts? Is it easier, to say, Thy sins be forgiven thee; or to say, Arise, and walk?"* Just to show them who He was and that He could forgive sins, He said to the sick man, *"Arise, take up thy bed, and go unto thine house,"* and the man did. The man got healed.

Notice that when Jesus said, *"That you may know that the Son of man has power (authority) on earth to forgive sin,"* He didn't say, "…the Son of God." Every time He said, *"The Son of man,"* He was always emphasizing his humanity, not His deity.

Go back to James 5:15, *"The prayer of faith shall save the sick and the Lord shall raise him up and if he hath committed sins, they shall be forgiven him."* He didn't say that you've got to root them out. He didn't say you can't get healed until you get rid of them. Sin will not stop your healing. Do you know what will stop it? You believing that sin will stop your healing is what will stop it. As I have said on our website, "The only hindrance to healing is the fact that people believe there are hindrances to healing."

You may have been raised to believe that sin can stop your healing. You may believe that if you've got sin in your life, God won't hear you, He won't touch you, or He won't help you. If you would be honest, you would know that that is not true, because you know that God was merciful and kind to you. He gave you things you didn't deserve when you knew you were in sin, even if you tried to hide it from everybody else. He was the only person you couldn't hide it from, yet He was still merciful; He still blessed you.

You might have been like me at one point where I said, "God, don't you know what's going on? Doesn't sin matter at all?" That is when He spoke to me and said "Yes, and I will deal with you later!" That's when I started wanting holiness. I had a real desire for holiness!

We need to realize that God is merciful. Should you be in sin? Of course not, but if you're raised and taught that sin stops the power of God, then why don't you just say that Satan is stronger? If sin is the nature and character of Satan and you say that sin can stop God, then you are saying that sin is more powerful than the power of God! If that were true, it would mean that sin is more powerful than righteousness, and that Adam's sin was greater than

Jesus' blood and forgiveness. We know that nothing is more powerful than the power of God!

People say, "I've been prayed for, so if I take my medicine will that stop the power of God from healing me?" I'm thinking, "That little pill? I don't think it's more powerful than the power of God!"

1 John 3:20-22,

> *20 For if our heart condemn us, God is greater than our heart, and knoweth all things.*
>
> *21 Beloved, if our heart condemn us not, then have we confidence toward God.*
>
> *22 And whatsoever we ask, we receive of him, because we keep his commandments, and do those things that are pleasing in his sight.*

Confidence toward God is faith toward God. Think about this: if your conscience condemns you, you have no confidence toward God, so you have no faith toward God. If you have no faith toward God, then you're not going to get anything from God, which means that you can't even get yourself healed. So many times when a person has sin in their life, it's not the sin that stops it; it's their conscience that stops it.

You know yourself, and you know that if you were God, you wouldn't heal you. What you're not taking into account is how you would feel about you if you were God. God knows you, and He still loves you. God loves you more than you love yourself. You might not think that is possible, but that is possible, and God does. However, if your conscience condemns you, then you will shrink back from God, and you won't have any faith toward Him.

This is what helped me see this: I would preach, and then we would have a healing line. People would come up and say different things to me like: "I've been prayed for by Benny Hinn," or "I've been prayed for by Oral Roberts." It was amazing how famous some of the people who had prayed for them were. I was thinking, "Wow, really? What was Oral like? I've never met him; what was he like?"

They would say, "There must be sin in my life." I would think: "If you really believe that the sin is going to stop the power of God then what are you doing in my healing line? If sin can stop the power of God, you are wasting your time getting in any healing line until you get the sin out of your life," yet people still lined up. Why? It was because inside they knew that it wasn't true, but their heads had been taught that it was. They would get up, and they would walk right up, like Abraham, hoping against hope. Inside they were thinking, "Somewhere maybe somebody has enough power to override this thing and get me free."

What I just described, having enough power to override a person's sin and get somebody free, is in Acts 10.

Acts 10:38,

> *38 How God anointed Jesus of Nazareth with the Holy Ghost and with power: who went about doing good, and healing all that were oppressed of the devil; for God was with him.*

That is the summary of Jesus' ministry. What He did overrode everything -- even a person's sin -- to bring about the will of God. Isn't that simple?

People would say to me, "I've got this thing, and I've got that thing." I would ask them, "Why don't you repent?" They would say, "Well, I have repented. I have done this, but I know I'm going to do it again." If you know you're going to do it again, you haven't really repented. What you've done is said that you're sorry, but that's like telling a person, "I'm sorry," and then you slap them in the face. These people would say, "Well, I've repented, but this thing has power over me." I would say, "No, it doesn't. We can break that, too."

I would pray for them, and they would be healed. They were amazed that they were healed with sin in their life. They would say, "I thought this sin would stop my healing." I would tell them: "No, that's not true. Sin doesn't stop the power of God. Unbelief stops the power of God, but your unbelief won't stop my faith."

Paul said, "Does your unbelief stop my faith? No. I can still have faith when you're in unbelief." Dr. Lake said the same thing. I've read so much about Dr. Lake, and sometimes, when people say certain things to me, I recall what Dr. Lake said.

People come up to me, and I ask, "What do you want me to do for you?" They say, "I don't know if you can do anything. I don't believe in healing; I believe it all passed away. I don't believe in laying hands on the sick. I don't believe in any of that." I ask, "What are you doing here?" I have heard, "I don't know. I figured it was my last hope. I figured I'd come and get prayed for."

Some ask, "Can you pray that the doctor will know what he's doing?" I get that all the time, too. I find myself thinking, "It's going to take more than a prayer." I tell people, "If you're going to go to the doctor, you had better have faith, because there are problems, and the statistics are not always good." There is a website I went to not long ago that had the statistics of all the different problems. It talked about what goes on in the medical field.

The amazing thing is that when you talk to these people, they will tell you that they don't have any faith and don't believe in healing. That's the sort of thinking they have. If I didn't believe in anything, I probably wouldn't show up at the meetings, but they still come in. I tell them, "It doesn't really matter what you believe; I believe."

Another thing they will come up and ask is: "Have you seen this disease healed?" Usually, that means that they have that disease; that's why they're asking. Most diseases we have seen healed, but there are some that I've never heard of. If they ask, "Have you ever seen this?" and I say, "What was that again? Hmm, no, I don't think so," they're going to say, "Oh, okay. Thank you." They think if you've never seen it healed, you never will. There's always a first time.

When you talk to these people, you have to watch how you answer. Instead of saying, "I've never seen that particular disease," I will ask, "Why?" They will say, "Because, that's what I've got." I say, "Well, let's pray." See how I just got around that? You say, "Isn't that kind of sneaky?" It's sneaky like Jesus. Did you ever notice that Jesus never answered anybody straight out?

These people come up, and they don't believe in anything. I'll tell them, "That's all right. I believe."

Dr. Lake had the same thing happen to him. Dr. Lake was sitting behind his desk and a man came in, and Dr. Lake asked, "What can I do for you? The man said, "I don't know if you can do anything. I don't believe in anything; I have no faith in doctors, I have no faith in man, and I have no faith in God." Dr. Lake pushed himself back and said, "That's all right. I've got enough faith for both of us." He got up and walked around to the side where the man was standing. As he stood there, he held the man's arm and talked to him. He wasn't even talking about God; he was just talking.

Dr. Lake asked him, "Can I pray for you?" "The man said I don't care what you do, but I'm a good Catholic, and I don't want anything that's going to hurt my religion." It's amazing the way people think. The man had a cane, and after a while, Dr. Lake took the cane and set it aside. He stood there just talking to him. After a few minutes, Dr. Lake shook the man's hand and he said, "Alright, you have a good day. May the Lord bless you." The man turned around and walked off without his cane, perfectly healed. He never even knew it had happened.

I'm going to quote what Dr. Lake said and make some of you mad, but you'll get excited anyway. Dr. Lake walked out into the hallway, and he called to the man.

The man's cane was still by his desk. He asked, "Do you want this cane?" and the man looked back into the door and said, "Oh, to hell with it!" The man walked on. The man was a Catholic who had no faith according to his own confession, yet he got healed.

I can't tell you how many people we've prayed for who were in the same situation. How can you tell how much faith a person has who is in a coma? I know that many times they're unconscious, but they're still conscious to some extent. They know what's going on around them a lot of times, but how do you know if they've got enough faith? It's amazing when you start analyzing these things. Most of it is just common sense, but unfortunately, common sense and religion don't usually run in the same circles.

James 5:16,

> *16 Confess your faults one to another, and pray one for another, that ye may be healed. The effectual fervent prayer of a righteous man availeth much.*

"Confess your faults one to another, and pray for one another that you may be healed." Notice that it doesn't say, "Unless God has got something else He wants to work out in your life, or unless God has got a better time, or unless there is something else hiding there." People put all kinds of things into that. No one in the Bible ever

put the qualifications in that people today put in, yet we build them up into some huge doctrine. We keep adding to them until they are huge, and they seem impossible to beat. It's not true, because they all have clay feet, and once you stomp their toe, the thing falls. It all simply comes back to what Jesus did. *"Jesus went about doing good and healing all that were oppressed of the devil."*

"The effectual fervent prayer of a righteous man availeth much." Notice: it was the *fervent prayer*. Praying the *fervent prayer* is the first thing you do. The average Christian will never see a healing in a hospital because the average Christian will not pray fervently in the hospital. Why? First of all, when a person goes into a hospital, they are going into the enemy's territory. The patient has hours and hours of death being fed or spoken to them. It is amazing how much pressure is put on the person who is going in to pray to conform to how things are done in there.

When you walk into a hospital, you start speaking in a whisper, automatically. You don't talk loud, and you don't talk strong. You don't go in there and stand at one end of the hall and shout, "Hallelujah." You don't do any of that. Why? That's because you want to be respectful. The same atmosphere that's in the hospital is also found in two other places: the church and the funeral home. It's the same attitude. If you go in and assume the same position of death, and fear, and submit to that thing, then you're not going to get results; you're not going to pray fervently.

You've got to go in there and be able to pray fervently. The word *fervent* means *white hot*. Another way would be almost like an argument, being strong and forceful. That's why most people who pray in hospitals never pray a strong and forceful prayer. Why? They don't want to get kicked out. In a hospital, you get to pray one fervent prayer, and then you're escorted out. Usually, that's the way it is, so you have to learn to pray forcefully, and yet do it quietly.

You can do that, but it does take some practice. You have to be able to release the power of God with force and not volume. When you start, volume usually equals power, because you stir yourself up. I'm not going to tell you how much time it will take you to build up to that, because it is up to you how much you practice. When I say practice, I mean actually doing it. I don't mean standing in front of a mirror at home practicing. I mean really doing it.

Today people take the word for practice to mean to *play like*. When I was in martial arts practice meant that I was fixing to sweat. It didn't mean that I was going to go and *play like* I was fighting; it meant that I was going to work, and practice, and train.

Notice: it was the fervent prayers of a righteous man, not the fervent prayers of a heathen.

First of all, heathens won't pray fervent prayers, because their conscience condemns them.

Secondly, they don't know how to pray fervent prayers, because for lack of a better term, they're going to pray the wrong way. They're going to pray begging prayers. We are never promised answers to begging prayers.

Nowhere in the Bible, in the New Testament especially, are you ever told to ask God for any type of healing, or for God to heal a person, or for God to cast a devil out of a person. I've heard that all of my life: "Oh, Lord, cast the devil out of this person, and set them free!" Sometimes, out of the mercy of God, the person is healed. Personally, I think the person who was praying had faith to rise up to a point where they could actually say it in faith, and then it happened. In reality, if God really answered the words of your prayer, nothing would happen. That's because He said, "You cast out devils, you heal the sick, and you preach the Gospel."

If you're going to pray and ask God to heal so and so, or touch so and so, or cast that devil out of them, then you also have to say, "God, preach the Gospel," because it's all the same. If He's not going to preach the Gospel to every creature, that is Him personally show up and do it, then He's also not going to show up personally and cast out every devil and heal everyone who is sick.

If God tells you to do something, He's not going to do it. He's going to do it <u>through</u> you. You're not going to stand back and expect Him to do what He has already told you to do. If He's not going to preach the Gospel and you've still got to preach the Gospel, then He's not going to cast out the devil; you've got to do it. If you beg him to do it, that's an unanswered prayer. At some point, you've got to step up and do your job.

Mark 3:1-6,

> *1 And he entered again into the synagogue; and there was a man there which had a withered hand.*
>
> *2 And they watched him, whether he would heal him on the sabbath day; that they might accuse him.*
>
> *3 And he saith unto the man which had the withered hand, Stand forth.*
>
> *4 And he saith unto them, Is it lawful to do good on the sabbath days, or to do evil? to save life, or to kill? But they held their peace.*
>
> *5 And when he had looked round about on them with anger, being grieved for the hardness of their hearts, he saith unto the man, Stretch forth thine*

hand. And he stretched it out: and his hand was restored whole as the other.

6 And the Pharisees went forth, and straightway took counsel with the Herodians against him, how they might destroy him.

"*And he entered again into the synagogue* [speaking of Jesus] *and there was a man there which had a withered hand. And they watched Him* [Jesus]..." Now, think about this: here was a man who was sitting there with a withered hand and all the Pharisees were looking around, and they were all watching Jesus. They knew what He was going to do.

Wouldn't you like a reputation like that? "Step back! There is a guy in a wheelchair, and when that preacher gets here, watch what happens!" That's the reputation I want! Amen? That's how consistent and systematic He was. It wasn't hit or miss. If it had been just hit or miss, then they wouldn't have thought like that at all. It wouldn't have mattered because it was too hit and miss. However, because He did it so consistently, there was no question in the minds of those religious people that Jesus was going to heal the man. They only had one question: "Is He going to do it on the Sabbath and violate one of our laws?"

I was writing a book on some of the sacred cows. I started reading in Timothy where it says, *"In the end times, people are not going to stand with sound doctrine, but people having itching ears are going to heap to themselves teachers who are going to teach fables."* I looked up the word *fable* in the Greek, and it means: *a myth or a superstition.* We call these fables: "Sacred cows." The word for *fable* in the Greek is the word *muthos* (pronounced moo'thos). I am not kidding. I was shocked. I got so excited, because I used to tell people, "When you hear a sacred cow being taught, you in the congregation ought to do a moooo." Now when you do it, what you will really be saying is, "Fable!"

"They watched Him, whether He would heal him on the Sabbath day."

"And He said unto the man which had the withered hand, Stand forth."

"And He said unto them…" which meant that Jesus was speaking to all of those religious people who were watching Him.

Jesus wasn't talking to the man when He asked, *"Is it lawful to do good on the Sabbath days, or to do evil?"* He had told the man, *"Stand forth,"* and the man stood up. Then Jesus spoke to all of those religious people and said, *"Is it lawful to do good on the Sabbath days, or to do evil?"*

To the man, Jesus was saying, "Stand here. I'll be back with you in a minute. I'm making a point out of you." If you'll be specific in the wording and look at what was actually written, it's amazing how the Word opens up.

In Mark 16:18 it says, *"Believers shall lay hands on the sick, and they shall recover."* The sick are the ones who shall recover. The believer is the one laying hands which means that believers shouldn't be sick. That means there are two categories in God's mind: there are believers, and there are sick people. We need to realize that we ought to be the ones who are well, and as we lay hands on the sick, they will recover.

"Jesus said unto them, 'Is it lawful to do good on the sabbath days, or to do evil? to save life, or to kill?' But they held their peace."

Why did the Pharisees hold their peace? That's because they knew they were wrong.

"And when He had looked round about on them with anger..." Look! Jesus got angry. Imagine that!

"Being grieved for the hardness of their hearts, He says unto the man, 'stretch forth your hand.'" Notice that the man had a withered hand and it wouldn't stretch forth,

but when Jesus said, *"Stretch forth your hand,"* the man did it, and his hand was healed.

"And he stretched it out: and his hand was restored whole as the other."

The point here is that Jesus never said anything to this man about having faith? He didn't ask, "How much faith do you have?" He didn't stand up and say, "You will be healed according to your faith." He didn't say any of that. As a matter of fact, He said, *"Come here, and stand,"* and the man came up and Jesus had him to stand there for a second. Then Jesus turned his attention away from the man to the Pharisees, and He said, *"Is it lawful to do good or to do evil?"* Then Jesus went back and did good, and He healed the man.

If it had been the man who had had faith, Jesus would have said that the man had faith to be healed. Jesus obviously healed the man by His own faith or else the Pharisees would have gotten angry at the man who was healed for having faith on the Sabbath. Instead, they got angry at Jesus, which meant that Jesus' faith healed the man. *"Whatsoever is not of faith is sin."* Jesus didn't sin, so Jesus had to walk in faith. Somebody had to use faith. Whose faith was used here? It wasn't the man's faith. The Pharisees saw whose faith was used here, and that's what they got angry about. Faith healed the man. In James, it says, *"The prayer of faith saves the sick."*

Faith healed the man, and we have determined that Jesus had the faith. If the man had had faith, the Pharisees would have been angry at the wrong person.

We find the same story in Luke.

Luke 6:6-11,

> *6 And it came to pass also on another sabbath, that he entered into the synagogue and taught: and there was a man whose right hand was withered.*
>
> *7 And the scribes and Pharisees watched him, whether he would heal on the sabbath day; that they might find an accusation against him.*
>
> *8 But he knew their thoughts, and said to the man which had the withered hand, Rise up, and stand forth in the midst. And he arose and stood forth.*
>
> *9 Then said Jesus unto them, I will ask you one thing; Is it lawful on the sabbath days to do good, or to do evil? to save life, or to destroy it?*
>
> *10 And looking round about upon them all, he said unto the man, Stretch forth thy hand. And he did so: and his hand was restored whole as the other.*
>
> *11 And they were filled with madness; and communed one with another what they might do to Jesus.*

Now, can you imagine people that religious? They would get so mad to be proven wrong just because He was violating one of their traditions. We've seen that happen before. It's amazing how the Pharisee spirit is still alive and well. It will still kill you if it gets the chance.

Mark 3:9-15,

> *9 And he spake to his disciples, that a small ship should wait on him because of the multitude, lest they should throng him.*
>
> *10 For he had healed many; insomuch that they pressed upon him for to touch him, as many as had plagues.*
>
> *11 And unclean spirits, when they saw him, fell down before him, and cried, saying, Thou art the Son of God.*
>
> *12 And he straitly charged them that they should not make him known.*
>
> *13 And he goeth up into a mountain, and calleth unto him whom he would: and they came unto him.*
>
> *14 And he ordained twelve, that they should be with him, and that he might send them forth to preach,*

15 And to have power to heal sicknesses, and to cast out devils:

Notice: *"Jesus ordained twelve, that they should be with Him, and that He might send them forth to preach."* He was saying, "Come and be with me." **The heart of discipleship is that you pour into a person everything that you are so that they can become better than you.** Isn't that amazing? In other words, they become better than you, by you giving them everything you have. That's the way it's supposed to be.

Here Jesus was saying, "You come with Me. The reason I want you with Me is because I'm going to send you out to preach." I've got to get this point across to you, because you've got to see this. He ordained twelve that they should be with Him, and that He might send them forth to preach, and that they should have power to heal sicknesses and cast out devils.

You will never find a place where Jesus ordained or sent someone out that He didn't at the same time give them power over sickness, disease, and devils; not one time. He never said for them just to preach. He never said that. He ordained the twelve to be with Him so He could send them out to preach, heal the sick, and cast out devils. In other words, *"I want you to do the same thing I'm doing."*

Now, if you cannot have faith for another person, this whole thing about having power over devils, sickness, and disease is useless; it means nothing. If you can't have power over those things, why do you need it? You don't need power, if they have faith. If faith will heal them, why do you need power to go over their faith? That's because they can get power straight from God to set themselves free.

Luke 13:10-16,

> *10 And he was teaching in one of the synagogues on the sabbath.*
>
> *11 And, behold, there was a woman which had a spirit of infirmity eighteen years, and was bowed together, and could in no wise lift up herself.*
>
> *12 And when Jesus saw her, he called her to him, and said unto her, Woman, thou art loosed from thine infirmity.*
>
> *13 And he laid his hands on her: and immediately she was made straight, and glorified God.*

"Behold, there was a woman who had a spirit of infirmity eighteen years, and was bowed together, and could in no wise lift herself up, and when Jesus saw her, He called her to Him, and said unto her, 'Woman, thou art loosed from thine infirmity.'" Notice that it doesn't say, "When

the Spirit said unto Him," or "When He was led by the Spirit," or "When the Spirit gave Him a rhema word to go and lay hands on her." You don't see any of that. He walked into the synagogue, and He saw her. It says, *"When He saw her,"* not when He knew something, *"He called her to Him."* It doesn't say that He had a word from God, a vision, a prophecy, a confirmation, or any of that.

In the book of Revelation, it says that any person who adds to this book or takes away from this Book will have their name blotted out. It would be good if we took that same verse and put it at the end of every chapter. Religious people are constantly adding to or taking something out of the Word of God. At some point, they have to get back to just what it says.

Some will say, "What you don't understand is that Jesus was so spiritual that He knew things instantly." I have heard people preach it that way. What Bible do they have? That is not in my Bible. They say, "You have to understand that Jesus had the Spirit of God without measure, and so He just knew everything." If that were the case, then He is not my example. If He had all of this secret knowledge and didn't have to operate by faith, then He is not my example, because I have to operate by faith, and I don't have all of that secret knowledge.

Why do people think that they have to add something to the Word? They do if they are going to build up all of the other doctrines that they have built upon the traditions of man.

In reality all it says is, *"When He saw her…"* If there is a crowd of people in a church and you walk in, what is the first thing you do? You look around to see who is there. You have the men on one side and the women on the other side, like it was back then. You see this one little woman who is bent over. You hear somebody ask, "Well, Miriam, how are you doing?" She says, "I'm doing fine. Who is that?" because she can't even look up to see who is speaking. When Jesus saw her, what do you think He was thinking? Do you think He heard a voice out of heaven say, "Jesus, thou Son of God, set this woman free"? It doesn't say He heard anything. It says, *"He laid His hands on her: and immediately she was made straight, and glorified God."*

Now watch this:

> *14 And the ruler of the synagogue answered with indignation, because that Jesus had healed on the sabbath day, and said unto the people, There are six days in which men ought to work: in them therefore come and be healed, and not on the sabbath day.*

> *15 The Lord then answered him, and said, Thou hypocrite, doth not each one of you on the sabbath loose his ox or his ass from the stall, and lead him away to watering?*

"*And the ruler of the synagogue answered.*" Answered? Nobody was talking to him. Nobody even said anything to him. Do you know what he answered? He answered the healing. He answered the healing "*with indignation,*" because Jesus healed this woman on the Sabbath.

In the military, they sometimes fire what they call a salvo. A big battleship will pull up, have the cannons out, and fire a salvo. Then the other side will answer and fire back. They are answering one salvo with another salvo; they are answering their attacker. That's what was going on here. Jesus fired offensively against the enemy, and the enemy answered back.

The enemy didn't answer back with power, because he doesn't have any power. What did he try to do? He tried to reinforce a stronghold. He tried to reinforce a tradition of man to try to answer the attack that the son of God had just launched onto his kingdom. "*He answered with indignation because that Jesus had healed on the Sabbath day, and said unto the people, 'There are six days in which men ought to work.'*" This woman had been like that for *eighteen* years! This Pharisee couldn't find one of those six days in all of those *eighteen* years that he worked to help this woman. He had to wait until Jesus showed up on an off day and do something outside of their tradition.

Rather than saying, "Wow, people, did you see that? Miriam has been like that for *eighteen* years. She is glorifying God. Let us join with her, and let us glorify God." He didn't do that. He turned around and said, "This is not right." Why? That's because the Pharisee had been there for *eighteen* years preaching, and Jesus walked in the first day and set the woman free.

The Pharisee had to answer for that somehow. Why? He saw that he was going to lose his position. They were going to walk up to him and say, "Who are you? We're going to follow this other guy." If the Pharisee had said, "But he is not right," they would have said, "He healed Miriam." If the Pharisee had said, "Just because there was a healing, it doesn't mean you ought to follow Him," then they would have said, "Ask Miriam."

Isn't that what the blind man said? (John 9:24-25). The Pharisees said to him, *"Give God the praise: we know that this Man [Jesus] is a sinner."* The blind man answered and said, *"Whether He be a sinner or no, I know not: one thing I know, that, whereas I was blind, now I see."* That's a pretty good answer. Amen?

Notice it says that the ruler of the synagogue was talking to the people, but he was also talking to the woman. He was getting to her at the same time. He said, *"There are six days in which people ought to work, in them come to be healed, and not on the Sabbath day."* In other words, "Woman, you shouldn't even have gotten healed." Notice what happened here, because when you really get into the story it is amazing. It says, *"Then the Lord answered him and said, 'You hypocrite.'"*

Think about it: this Pharisee was some kind of pastor. Then this new guy came in and did a healing and people got all excited, some good, some bad. Then the pastor said, "Now, wait. This isn't right. We don't agree with that." Then, the person who had just done it turned around and said, *"You hypocrite."* Can you imagine how that would go over in the church today? They would be calling security. They would call it rebellion. If that was rebellion, Jesus was in it.

> *16 And ought not this woman, being a daughter of Abraham, whom Satan hath bound, lo, these eighteen years, be loosed from this bond on the sabbath day?*

He said, *"You hypocrite, doth not each one of you on the Sabbath loose his ox or his ass from the stall and lead him away to water him? And ought not this woman, being a daughter of Abraham…"* Jesus just told you why

He did it. It wasn't because He heard a voice, it wasn't because He had a leading, and it wasn't because of anything other than the fact of who this woman was.

The Bible even tells us in Galatians 6:10, *"Let us do good unto all men, especially unto them who are of the household of faith."* Heal the sick everywhere you go, especially in the church, because the church ought to be well!

Jesus said, *"This woman whom Satan hath bound lo these eighteen years, be loosed from this bond on the Sabbath day."* Now, I don't know what that Pharisee had been telling the people all those years. He might have possibly told her, "Miriam, we know you're bound by Satan. One day, God's going to set you free. It will probably be on the year of Jubilee, but that isn't today."

Honestly, probably what had happened was that the Pharisee preached that sermon the Saturday before. He probably told her, "Don't worry Miriam, your day is coming. God is working all of this out in your life. If you would finally confess that sin that you've kept hidden these eighteen years, then this thing would be broken off of you, but you won't confess it." He might have said, "You don't have enough faith," or "We don't know what it is, but God knows, and some day, Miriam, you'll be free." Then, Jesus walked in, and when He saw her, He called her to Him, and said, *"Woman, you are loosed from your infirmity."*

Now think about this: suppose I came in here and there was a woman standing over in the corner who was bowed over. Maybe she was knotted up somehow and I said, "To the woman in the back there, come here." She might say, "Why do I have to come up there? Why don't you come back here to me?" This woman was bowed over, but she still had to walk to Jesus. It says that Jesus called her to Him, which means that He wasn't standing right in front of her. He had to call to her from across the room. He called her to Him and the woman had to walk to Him. Do you know what that must have looked like? She was bowed over, and she couldn't lift herself up. She had to walk all the way over to Him. When she got there, He said, *"Woman, you are loosed from your infirmity,"* and then it says, *"He laid His hands on her: and immediately she was made straight, and glorified God."*

What was Jesus doing when He laid His hands on her? He was declaring the justice of God (Psalm 103). Then He applied the power (ability) to set her free. That's called the Baptism of the Holy Spirit. Jesus had that, too. He called her over and said, *"You are loosed from your infirmity,"* and He set her free.

Notice that nowhere in there did He ask, "Woman, how much faith do you have?" It doesn't say that He called her to Him and said, "Woman, how do you feel today? Let's see how much faith you have, because I'm not sure how much faith I've got." No, he didn't say any of that.

Now, think about it: if her healing had depended on her faith, wouldn't it have been amazing if, all of a sudden, she had gotten faith right then to be healed? If she had had faith before, she would have gotten healed before then. For eighteen years she put up with it, and Jesus just happened to be there on the day that she had enough faith to get healed? That would have been something.

There was a guy who wrote on the website one time, and he said, "You're telling people that they can be healed. You're giving people false hope. The testimonies that you have of people being healed -- they probably would have been healed anyway. It probably was something that wasn't serious." I was thinking, "Terminal cancer, that's minor?" We had all of these different testimonies of people being healed. People had had these illnesses for years, we prayed, and the next day they were well, and it was just a coincidence? It's amazing how the human mind will try to rationalize.

There is no authority without responsibility. It's just like when you have children. You have authority over your children as long as you take responsibility for them. When you quit taking responsibility for them, the state will come in and take away your authority over them.

Authority comes with responsibility. If you want authority, take responsibility. *"Am I my brother's keeper?"* That's what it comes back to. When you start to take responsibility for other people, the authority is there.

There can be no authority without power. Authority without power is like a commandment without a command. If there's not a command behind it, it's a wish. A policeman does not have authority unless he has ability to back up what he tells you to do. His authority goes only as far as his power to back up what he says. Your authority goes only as far as your power to back up what you say.

You cannot separate responsibility from authority or authority from power. They're not all the same thing, but they're all connected. They are like a train. If you hook up to one, you've got the other one as well. That's why it's so funny to watch these people on TV. They try to sell you anointing, and power, and gifts. "Send in your money, and this anointing will come upon you." That's like selling you your own car. You already have it, and they're trying to sell it back to you.

Matthew 5:44,

> *44 But I say unto you, Love your enemies, bless them that curse you, do good to them that hate you, and*

> *pray for them which despitefully use you, and persecute you;*

Notice it says, "Love your enemies, bless them that curse you, do good to them that hate you."

Acts 10:38,

> *38 How God anointed Jesus of Nazareth with the Holy Ghost and with power: who went about doing good, and healing all that were oppressed of the devil; for God was with him.*

What did it say Jesus did? *"He went about doing good."* How did He do good? It was by healing all who were oppressed of the devil, so healing is doing good. Matthew 5:44 says to do good even to those who hate you, so it doesn't matter who it is. You are to have faith for them so you can set them free, no matter what.

John 18:10-11,

> *10 Then Simon Peter having a sword drew it, and smote the high priest's servant, and cut off his right ear. The servant's name was Malchus.*

> *11 Then said Jesus unto Peter, Put up thy sword into the sheath: the cup which my Father hath given me, shall I not drink it?*

Now, go down to Luke 22. I'm tying all of these together.

Luke 22:48-51,

> *48 But Jesus said unto him, Judas, betrayest thou the Son of man with a kiss?*
>
> *49 When they which were about him saw what would follow, they said unto him, Lord, shall we smite with the sword?*

We already know the story of how Peter smote the servant of the High Priest and cut off his right ear.

> *50 And one of them smote the servant of the high priest, and cut off his right ear.*
>
> *51 And Jesus answered and said, Suffer ye thus far. And he touched his ear, and healed him.*

It says, "And Jesus answered [Jesus said unto Peter]." What did He answer? He answered Peter's action: *"And He answered and said, 'Suffer ye thus far.' And He touched his ear, and healed him."* Who did Jesus heal? He healed the High Priest's servant who was His enemy, the one who came to arrest Him. Isn't that doing good to those who hate you, and wasn't He doing His own word in Matthew 5:44? *"I say unto you, 'Love your enemies, bless them that curse you, do good to them that hate you, and pray for them which despitefully use you, and persecute you.'"* That's what He was doing.

Now, can you imagine how this happened? This wasn't in some healing service; this didn't go on for hours. They came out, there was a lot of jostling around, and Judas kissed Him. They were taking Jesus away and Peter said, "Oh, no, you aren't!" and there went the ear! Jesus didn't have time to say anything to Malchus. He didn't say, "Malchus, if you will only believe, I can put that ear back on." Jesus didn't have time; they were dragging Him off.

Now, imagine this: here Jesus was; He was being arrested. If you're being arrested, your mind usually isn't focused on people. It's more focused on: "What time is my lawyer available?" or "Do you know where the nearest bail bondsman is?" You're not thinking in terms of doing good. You're thinking in terms of survival. In all of this jostling, it was like, "Wham!" and off came the ear, and Jesus never missed a beat. He put the ear back on. How much faith do you think Malchus had? There is no intimation of faith. There's no mention that Malchus had faith for the healing of his ear. He was coming to arrest Jesus. He didn't have faith in Jesus, but Jesus had faith for him. Why? Jesus had power.

We learned the story of the centurion in Matthew.

Matthew 8:5-7,

> *5 And when Jesus was entered into Capernaum, there came unto him a centurion, beseeching him,*
>
> *6 And saying, Lord, my servant lieth at home sick of the palsy, grievously tormented.*
>
> *7 And Jesus saith unto him, I will come and heal him.*

The centurion had a servant, and he came to Jesus and said *"Lord, my servant lieth at home sick,"* and Jesus said, *"I will come and heal him."* It was just that quick. He didn't say, "Hang on a minute; I have to get a word from God. Let me see if it's God's will. Maybe He won't get healed, because you're a heathen." He didn't say any of that. He just said, *"I will come and heal him."*

Luke 7:6-10,

> *6 Then Jesus went with them. And when he was now not far from the house, the centurion sent friends to him, saying unto him, Lord, trouble not thyself: for I am not worthy that thou shouldest enter under my roof:*
>
> *7 Wherefore neither thought I myself worthy to come unto thee: but say in a word, and my servant shall be healed.*

8 For I also am a man set under authority, having under me soldiers, and I say unto one, Go, and he goeth; and to another, Come, and he cometh; and to my servant, Do this, and he doeth it.

9 When Jesus heard these things, he marvelled at him, and turned him about, and said unto the people that followed him, I say unto you, I have not found so great faith, no, not in Israel.

10 And they that were sent, returning to the house, found the servant whole that had been sick.

Verse 6 says, *"Then Jesus went with them. And when He was now not far from the house, the centurion sent friends to Him, saying unto Him, Lord, trouble not Thyself: for I am not worthy that Thou shouldest enter under my roof."*

The centurion was saying, "No, Lord, understand that I'm not worthy that you should come under my roof. However, I am a man under authority, and I understand authority. I have men under me, and if I tell them to go, they will go, and if I tell them to come, they will come. I know that if you just tell this thing to go, it will go."

Do you realize that he understood authority to the point that he knew that Jesus had authority over sickness and disease? He could have said, "No, Lord, I know that you've got authority. I understand authority, and you don't have to come under my roof, but if you would send Peter, he could do it." We would think of the men under him as soldiers, so wouldn't the coming and going of Jesus' disciples be the equivalent of the centurion's solders?

The centurion was saying, "Say in a word, and my servant shall be healed. I understand that you've got authority over sickness and disease." Notice he never talked about the servant; he talked about the disease. He was saying, "If you tell it to go, it will go." Why? That's because he recognized that Jesus had authority over it.

I know this almost sounds like a contradiction, because we care about people, but people don't determine the healing. You want results because you want the people to live, but for a split second, get your mind off of the people, and recognize that this is an enemy to be driven out. Once you recognize that, it doesn't matter who the disease or enemy is. The faith level of the person doesn't matter. All that matters is that it is an enemy of God. We have authority over it, and it has to go.

Suppose a policeman goes to a person's house where there is a criminal. The policeman will say, "If you give me permission I'll come in." The person of the house asks, "Do you have a warrant to enter?" The policeman will say, "No, but if you don't give me permission, I'm going to get a warrant, and I will get one for you too, because you're aiding and abetting."

We put that back on Christians all the time. "Well, I opened the door." "Yes, then you were aiding and abetting. Repent." Even if you don't repent, I'm still going to cast it out, and you'll still be guilty. That is what people don't get.

The church today doesn't understand authority over sickness and disease, and authority over all the works of the enemy. It doesn't understand that at all. It thinks it has to do with a person's faith level and a person being good. Most people preach grace, but then they practice works. Works have nothing to do with it. It has to do with the fact that we have authority over sickness and disease, and over all the works of the enemy.

I'm going to give you examples of *third party healings*. Remember what Jesus said about the centurion?

Matthew 8:10,

> *10 When Jesus heard it, he marvelled, and said to them that followed, Verily I say unto you, I have not found so great faith, no, not in Israel.*

When Jesus talked to the people around Him about the centurion, He said, *"I have not found so great faith, no, not in Israel."* Who had the faith? Who got the servant healed? Was it the centurion's faith or Jesus' faith? It was the centurion's faith, right? That was a third party healing. You had the servant who got healed, the centurion who had faith, and Jesus who provided the power. We still have Jesus today who provides the power, and you've got the faith for whomever. When you understand that, it is amazing!

I've heard this preached exactly the opposite using the same people. They'll tell you that if you want to be healed, you've got to have your own faith to be healed. This centurion had faith. The centurion wasn't sick. It was his servant who was sick.

Matthew 15:22-28,

> *22 And, behold, a woman of Canaan came out of the same coasts, and cried unto him, saying, Have mercy on me, O Lord, thou Son of David; my daughter is grievously vexed with a devil.*
>
> *23 But he answered her not a word. And his disciples came and besought him, saying, Send her away; for she crieth after us.*
>
> *24 But he answered and said, I am not sent but unto the lost sheep of the house of Israel.*
>
> *25 Then came she and worshipped him, saying, Lord, help me.*

26 But he answered and said, It is not meet to take the children's bread, and to cast it to dogs.

27 And she said, Truth, Lord: yet the dogs eat of the crumbs which fall from their masters' table.

28 Then Jesus answered and said unto her, O woman, great is thy faith: be it unto thee even as thou wilt. And her daughter was made whole from that very hour.

Matthew 15:22, *"And, behold, a woman of Canaan came out of the same coasts, and cried unto Him, saying, 'Have mercy on me, Lord.'"* Notice: she cried, *"Have mercy on me."* It doesn't say she asked for Him to have mercy on her daughter. She said, *"Have mercy on me, Lord."* She went on to tell Him, *"Thou son of David; my daughter is grievously vexed with a devil."* Honestly, that's exactly the way it is. When your child is sick, yes the child is having problems, but I guarantee you that when you want your child healed you say, "God have mercy on me," because nothing hurts you more than watching your child have a problem.

Now, who was the sick person here? Who had the devil? The daughter was the sick person who had the devil. Who was the one with faith? The mother of the sick girl, the woman of Canaan, had the faith. Who had the power? Jesus had the power. It was the same scenario; it was *third party healing.* What does that mean? The woman of Canaan had faith for somebody else, and the centurion had faith for somebody else.

Mark 9:24-27,

> *24 And straightway the father of the child cried out, and said with tears, Lord, I believe; help thou mine unbelief.*
>
> *25 When Jesus saw that the people came running together, he rebuked the foul spirit, saying unto him, Thou dumb and deaf spirit, I charge thee, come out of him, and enter no more into him.*
>
> *26 And the spirit cried, and rent him sore, and came out of him: and he was as one dead; insomuch that many said, He is dead.*
>
> *27 But Jesus took him by the hand, and lifted him up; and he arose.*

"Straightway the father of the child cried out, and said with tears, 'Lord, I believe; help thou mine unbelief.'" We know this story. First of all the man brought his son to Jesus' disciples. They tried to cast the devil out, but they couldn't do it.

That is when the church would have said, "Oh, it must not be God's will," or if the church had advanced past that to where it was God's will, then there must have been a sin in the father. They would have seen it as getting passed down, so it must have been the father's fault. The church, however, hasn't progressed past that yet. It's still there.

There is another account of this same story in Matthew 17.

Matthew 17:17,

> *17 Then Jesus answered and said, O faithless and perverse generation, how long shall I be with you? how long shall I suffer you? bring him hither to me.*

The disciples couldn't cast the devil out, so what did Jesus say? Jesus said, *"You faithless and perverse generation, how long do I have to put up with you."* He was talking to His own disciples. Why? That's because they couldn't get it done, so they brought the boy to Him. Notice that the father said, *"Lord, I believe; help Thou my unbelief."* In other words, *"I'm trying, I believe it, and I'm here. I brought my son to your disciples."* Isn't that the equivalent of James calling for the elders?

There were three people: the boy, the boy's father, and Jesus. The boy had a devil. We don't know that he didn't have faith, but we do know that he had a devil.

There is no mention of his faith. The father said, *"Lord, I believe; help Thou my unbelief,"* so he was a person with faith but with unbelief mixed in.

There was Jesus, the Provider of power, there was the father who was believing, even though he had some unbelief, and there was the son who got healed.

Luke 6:30,

> *30 Give to every man that asketh of thee; and of him that taketh away thy goods ask them not again.*

I ask people all the time, "What do you want me to do for you?" That is what Jesus asked. When I have a healing service, those are the exact words I use. People tell me, "Well, I've got this problem, and it started when I was four." I'll say, "No, I'm not asking you for your medical history. What do you want me to do for you?" They say, "Well, I want to be healed." Then I'll say, "Ok, what is the problem?" They say, "Well, I've got this disease." I'll say, "Alright, let me see your hands." Then I just minister.

That's what Jesus did. He asked, *"What do you want that I should do unto you?"* They said, *"I want to receive my sight."* He said, *"Receive your sight."* What happened? They got healed. That's all I'm doing. I'm just following His pattern. Why? That's because it isn't up to their faith; it's up to my faith. Now, if I didn't have faith, I would hope that they did. Somebody's got to have faith. I can have it, they can have it, or we can both have it. However, if neither one of us has it, it isn't going to happen.

Matthew 7:12,

> *12 Therefore all things whatsoever ye would that men should do to you, do ye even so to them: for this is the law and the prophets.*

Notice: Jesus was saying, "Do to them what you would want done to you."

Luke 10:25-37,

> *25 And, behold, a certain lawyer stood up, and tempted him, saying, Master, what shall I do to inherit eternal life?*
>
> *26 He said unto him, What is written in the law? how readest thou?*
>
> *27 And he answering said, Thou shalt love the Lord thy God with all thy heart, and with all thy soul, and with all thy strength, and with all thy mind; and thy neighbour as thyself.*
>
> *28 And he said unto him, Thou hast answered right: this do, and thou shalt live.*

29 But he, willing to justify himself, said unto Jesus, And who is my neighbour?

30 And Jesus answering said, A certain man went down from Jerusalem to Jericho, and fell among thieves, which stripped him of his raiment, and wounded him, and departed, leaving him half dead.

31 And by chance there came down a certain priest that way: and when he saw him, he passed by on the other side.

32 And likewise a Levite, when he was at the place, came and looked on him, and passed by on the other side.

You will notice it says that when the priest and the Levite saw him, they passed by on the other side. When Jesus saw the woman, what did He do? He called her to Him. That was the difference in their hearts.

33 But a certain Samaritan, as he journeyed, came where he was: and when he saw him, he had compassion on him,

34 And went to him, and bound up his wounds, pouring in oil and wine, and set him on his own beast, and brought him to an inn, and took care of him.

> *35 And on the morrow when he departed, he took out two pence, and gave them to the host, and said unto him, Take care of him; and whatsoever thou spendest more, when I come again, I will repay thee.*
>
> *36 Which now of these three, thinkest thou, was neighbour unto him that fell among the thieves?*
>
> *37 And he said, He that shewed mercy on him. Then said Jesus unto him, Go, and do thou likewise.*

"But a certain Samaritan saw him, and he had compassion on him." (Remember: the Jews didn't have any dealings with Samaritans; they disagreed.)

You may ask, "Am I my brother's keeper?" Yes. That's what Jesus was trying to get across. It's not what you say you are; it's what you do with who you are. It wasn't based on who the priest or the Samaritan were. It was based on what the person did. Jesus even said at one point: *"Not everyone who says Lord, Lord, will enter into the Kingdom of God but he that does the will of My Father."*

Genesis 20:1-7,

> *1 And Abraham journeyed from thence toward the south country, and dwelled between Kadesh and Shur, and sojourned in Gerar.*

> *2 And Abraham said of Sarah his wife, She is my sister: and Abimelech king of Gerar sent, and took Sarah.*
>
> *3 But God came to Abimelech in a dream by night, and said to him, Behold, thou art but a dead man, for the woman which thou hast taken; for she is a man's wife.*

Now that is a scary dream when God says you're a dead man! That's not a good dream.

> *4 But Abimelech had not come near her: and he said, Lord, wilt thou slay also a righteous nation?*
>
> *5 Said he not unto me, She is my sister? and she, even she herself said, He is my brother: in the integrity of my heart and innocency of my hands have I done this.*

In other words, "I didn't know; that's what they told me."

> *6 And God said unto him in a dream, Yea, I know that thou didst this in the integrity of thy heart; for I also withheld thee from sinning against me: therefore suffered I thee not to touch her.*
>
> *7 Now therefore restore the man his wife; for he is a prophet, and he shall pray for thee, and thou shalt live: and if thou restore her not, know thou that thou shalt surely die, thou, and all that are thine.*

If you go down to verse 17 it says,

> *17 So Abraham prayed unto God: and God healed Abimelech, and his wife, and his maidservants; and they bare children.*

Here was Abimelech who was a heathen king. Abraham being a man of God not only prayed for Abimelech, but he prayed for Abimelech's wife and her maidservants. All of them were barren, and then they all bore children. Here was the faith of a righteous man praying for the heathen, and God healed the heathen womb. Can a person have faith for another? Yes, even all the way back to Abraham. We see it all the way through.

In Matthew 9 and in Mark 5, it talks about how Jesus raised the ruler's daughter.

Over and over again, we see *third person faith*.

Luke 7:11-16,

> *11 And it came to pass the day after, that he went into a city called Nain; and many of his disciples went with him, and much people.*
>
> *12 Now when he came nigh to the gate of the city, behold, there was a dead man carried out, the only son of his mother, and she was a widow: and much people of the city was with her.*

13 And when the Lord saw her, he had compassion on her, and said unto her, Weep not.

14 And he came and touched the bier: and they that bare him stood still. And he said, Young man, I say unto thee, Arise.

15 And he that was dead sat up, and began to speak. And he delivered him to his mother.

16 And there came a fear on all: and they glorified God, saying, That a great prophet is risen up among us; and, That God hath visited his people.

Do you see that the dead man had no faith, and the woman had no faith? Jesus said, *"Woman, weep not."* He had compassion on her. It didn't even say that He had faith here, but we know He had faith, because He operated in faith. What moved Him though was compassion. It was not a word from God, and it was not a prophecy. Jesus saw her and had compassion. To say that He felt sorry for her is the best way to say it, so He turned around and gave her son back to her.

Here, Jesus was having faith for somebody else. It wasn't even for the young man. He didn't say, "Oh, it's so wrong that a young person die." He had compassion on the woman who was a widow; she shouldn't have had to lose her son. He had compassion on her, and He raised her son from the dead. Now think about that. We know the times where Jesus had compassion on the people and healed them, but it doesn't even say that He had compassion for the young man. It says that He had compassion on the woman; He had compassion that raised the dead. *"And he that was dead sat up, and began to speak."* When you talk about *third party healing*, that was a pretty good one there.

It was the same thing for Lazarus. Lazarus had no faith; he was dead. None of the people there had faith for him to be raised. They all thought they were going to see him again in the resurrection.

John 11:20-25,

> *20 Then Martha, as soon as she heard that Jesus was coming, went and met him: but Mary sat still in the house.*
>
> *21 Then said Martha unto Jesus, Lord, if thou hadst been here, my brother had not died.*
>
> *22 Then I know, that even now, whatsoever thou wilt ask of God, God will give it thee.*
>
> *23 Jesus saith unto her, Thy brother shall rise again.*
>
> *24 Martha saith unto him, I know that he shall rise again in the resurrection at the last day.*

HAVING FAITH FOR OTHERS

25 Jesus said unto her, I am the resurrection, and the life: he that believeth in me, though he were dead, yet shall he live:

Jesus was saying, "You don't get it. I am the resurrection. You don't have to wait until the end. I'll give it to you now." They didn't believe; nobody there had faith for Lazarus to get up. They had faith for Jesus to heal him while he was still alive, because Martha had said, *"We know that if You had been here he wouldn't have died."*

The faith of another person can raise the dead, but it wasn't Lazarus' faith, and it wasn't the faith of Lazarus' sisters. There wasn't a whole lot of faith there for raising the dead.

The problem with most of the faith teaching today is that they say, "Well, you've got to have faith in your own faith." No, you don't. You have to have faith in God. If you're having faith in your own faith, you're having faith in you. You might say, "Well, I don't know if I have enough faith." So what? Nobody in the Bible ever said, "I don't know if I have enough faith." The closest you can get is where the man said, *"Lord, I believe; help my unbelief."* You never saw people saying that to Jesus, and you never saw Jesus asking, "How much faith do you have?"

The last one is Jesus at the pool of Bethesda. It is a *second party faith.*

John 5:1-9,

> *1 After this there was a feast of the Jews; and Jesus went up to Jerusalem.*
>
> *2 Now there is at Jerusalem by the sheep market a pool, which is called in the Hebrew tongue Bethesda, having five porches.*
>
> *3 In these lay a great multitude of impotent folk, of blind, halt, withered, waiting for the moving of the water.*
>
> *4 For an angel went down at a certain season into the pool, and troubled the water: whosoever then first after the troubling of the water stepped in was made whole of whatsoever disease he had.*
>
> *5 And a certain man was there, which had an infirmity thirty and eight years.*
>
> *6 When Jesus saw him lie, and knew that he had been now a long time in that case, he saith unto him, Wilt thou be made whole?*

Notice again the same wording. *"When Jesus saw him…"* I've heard people talk about how Jesus walked along and heard the Spirit of God say to go up in there and look around. They say that He saw this person, then stepped over another person, and went around this other person to get to this one person. None of that's there. It just says, *"When Jesus saw him…"*

Now watch this: *"When Jesus saw him lie, and knew…"* It doesn't say how He knew, but He knew that the man had been there for a long time. Now, it wouldn't take long to know that. How many of you have visited somebody in the hospital? Just by walking into their room you can usually tell if they've been there a day, a week, or a month. The longer they're there, the more that room looks like a house. They have all kinds of different things in there. This man probably had his whole house built up around him.

> *7 The impotent man answered him, Sir, I have no man, when the water is troubled, to put me into the pool: but while I am coming, another steppeth down before me.*
>
> *8 Jesus saith unto him, Rise, take up thy bed, and walk.*
>
> *9 And immediately the man was made whole, and took up his bed, and walked: and on the same day was the sabbath.*

Notice: Jesus ignored the man and didn't answer his complaints. Then it says, *"Jesus saith unto him, 'Rise, take up thy bed, and walk.' And immediately the man was made whole, and took up his bed, and walked."* There was no mention of faith. Jesus was asking the person if he wanted to be healed, and then the person said, *"I don't have a man to help."* Could that be classified as faith? If so, everybody you talked to would have it. Somebody had faith for this man, and apparently it was Jesus. It was *second party faith*, somebody having faith for somebody else.

I hope I have proven my case that you can have faith for other people. I've enjoyed it, and I hope you have, too.

HAVING FAITH FOR OTHERS

- You are left unsatisfied by the status quo...
- You know you were meant to be a participant and not just a spectator...
- You ask "Why not?..." more than "Why?"...
- You believe that today can be better than yesterday...
- You know you were meant to walk among the Giants of the Faith, and you want the tools & training that can make it happen...
- When you hear the exploits of God's Generals, you can picture yourself doing them...

If this describes you, then you ARE JGLM... whether you know it or not.

COME.
LET'S CHANGE THE WORLD.

John G. Lake Ministries
SAME MESSAGE. SAME POWER. SAME RESULTS.

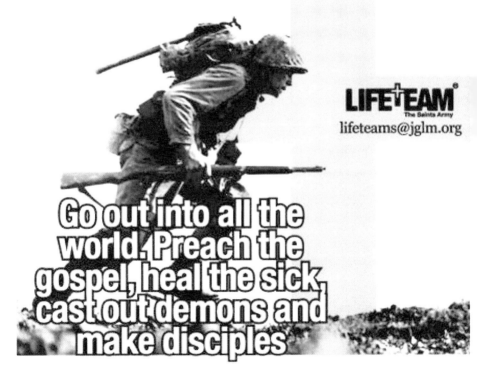

LIFE TEAM
The Saints Army
lifeteams@jglm.org

Go out into all the world. Preach the gospel, heal the sick, cast out demons and make disciples

John G. Lake Ministries
SAME MESSAGE. SAME POWER. SAME RESULTS.

PARTNER WITH US AS WE ADVANCE GOD'S KINGDOM ON EARTH!

Partner Benefits Include:

- Our monthly "Laboring Together" newsletter with a ministry update directly from Brother Curry that includes detailed information about our upcoming events and activities. We compile testimonies from all over the world to encourage and strengthen your faith.

- Partner E-Newsletter includes an MP3 every month taught by Brother Curry with the option to download our monthly audio teaching.

- 30% Discount on all products during the holiday season...

- Our Promise to Protect Your Kingdom Investment.

Partners can choose to receive packets by postal mail or via email. Your faithful support allows us to help give our materials away freely to those who cannot give, such as our JGLM prison ministries, disaster relief funds and foreign missionaries. Most importantly we depend on our faithful partners as our main line of prayer support.

Email: partners@jglm.org
www.jglm.org/partners

The Teaching That Birthed A Legend Is Now Raising An Army.

Get Yours Today
Call **888-293-6591**
or Visit Us Online
store.jglm.org

John G. Lake Ministries
SAME MESSAGE. SAME POWER. SAME RESULTS.

Glory to God, Freedom for All!

Join us online every Sunday at 10am:
broadcast.jglm.org
To learn more about Dominion Life visit:
jglm.org/dominion-life-church
or email: dliac@jglm.org

Church Membership Requirements

1. Must confess Jesus as Lord and that you are saved and born again.

2. Must at least be seeking and expecting to be filled with the Holy Spirit in accordance with Acts Chapter 2 (speaking with other tongues).

3. Must agree with the JGLM/IAC Statement of Faith, obtained by emailing us at: dliac@jglm.org.

4. You agree to pray for us according to the prayer directives that we will send to all church members on a regular basis.

5. You agree to support the church through tithes and offerings. Tithes and offerings must be sent to the church address and MUST be noted as Tithes/Offerings.

6. You agree to work towards becoming a certified DHT. Our hope is that ALL DLIAC members work toward becoming a certified DHT to advance the kingdom through this body. For information on becoming a DHT contact us by email at: iac@jglm.org or you can find all information on our website at www.jglm.org.

7. You agree to remain in the unity of the Spirit by living a life in accordance with the constitution and bylaws of the I.A.C.